A Kid's Guide to
INCREDIBLE TECHNOLOGY™

The Incredible Story of Aircraft Carriers

Greg Roza

PowerKids Press
New York

For Nick

Published in 2004 by The Rosen Publishing Group, Inc.
29 East 21st Street, New York, NY 10010

First Edition

Editor: Kathy Kuhtz Campbell
Book Design: Mike Donnellan

Illustration Credits: Leonello Calvetti, Lorenzo Cecchi
Photo Credits: pp. 4, 7 © Bettmann/CORBIS; p. 8 © CORBIS; p. 11 © George Hall/CORBIS; p. 12 © AFP/CORBIS; p. 16 © John Whalen/Newport News Shipbuilding; p. 20 © Courtesy of the Sea, Air and Space Museum.

Roza, Greg.
The incredible story of aircraft carriers / Greg Roza.— 1st ed.
     v. cm.— (A kid's guide to incredible technology)
Includes bibliographical references and index.
Contents: First carriers—Early airplanes—USS Enterprise—Parts of a carrier—Supercarriers—Another USS Enterprise—Building an aircraft carrier—The air wing—Flight operations—Aircraft carriers of the future.
  ISBN 0-8239-6714-X (library binding)
1. Aircraft carriers—United States—Juvenile literature. [1. Aircraft carriers.] I. Title. II. Series.
V874.3 .R68 2004
359.9'483'0973—dc21

                                                                      2002151444

Manufactured in the United States of America

Contents

First Carriers

Aircraft carriers, or carriers, are floating military airports used by the world's navies. These ships use modern **technology** to **transport** military aircraft and people around the world. Carriers have runways called flight decks, where planes take off and land.

The USS *Langley* was the first official aircraft carrier of the U.S. Navy, although some planes had taken off from and landed on naval ships before. The *Langley*, which was 534 feet (162.7 m) long, had been **converted** from the supply ship USS *Jupiter* in 1922. A wooden takeoff and landing surface was laid over its hull. The *Langley* ran pretend battles to test how useful it would be as a moving airport during a war. In 1927, the U.S. Navy converted two more ships into carriers, the USS *Lexington* and the USS *Saratoga*.

Top: *The USS* Saratoga *had a crew of about 2,000 people and carried about 81 airplanes.* Bottom: *The USS* Langley, *seen here in a 1922 photograph, had a crew of about 468 people and carried about 34 airplanes.*

Early Airplanes

In 1903, the Wright brothers made the first successful airplane flight near Kitty Hawk, North Carolina. Navies around the world soon realized that airplanes could be used for fighting battles. However, planes could not fly the great distances needed for their weapons to be useful. Navies built ships that could transport the planes to distant places. The first planes to be carried by ship during World War I (1914–1918) were **seaplanes**. These were lowered into the water from a ship, and they took off from the water. The first planes launched from ships, including the *Langley*, were **biplanes**. By 1939, **monoplanes** had succeeded biplanes. During World War II (1939–1945), many countries proved that planes launched from carriers could quickly approach enemy forces, attack with guns and bombs, and then return to the carrier.

Top: On December 17, 1903, with Orville Wright at the controls, the Flyer makes its first flight. The Wright brothers' biplane was made of spruce and ash and was covered with muslin, a cloth. Bottom: This illustration shows Eugene Ely in November 1910 taking off in a Curtiss biplane from the deck of the USS Birmingham, which was at anchor off the coast of Virginia. This was the first time a plane had been launched from a ship.

A runway on an aircraft carrier is not as long as a runway on the ground. Most early carriers had no more than 100 feet (30.5 m) for their takeoff surfaces. To help airplanes take off, early aircraft carriers sailed into the wind at high speeds. The early carriers could reach speeds of about 25 miles per hour (40.2 km/h).

The USS *Enterprise*

The carrier USS *Enterprise* began military service in May 1938. In 1941, Japan attacked the U.S. military base at Pearl Harbor, Hawaii, by using planes launched from Japanese aircraft carriers. This attack caused the United States to enter World War II officially. The U.S. Navy quickly improved the *Enterprise* for use in fighting the war. It replaced the carrier's guns with larger and more effective machine guns and cannons. The *Enterprise*'s **radar** system was replaced in late 1942 with one that was stronger and more exact. Its search radar could locate fighter planes flying 10,000 feet (3,048 m) high and 46 miles (74 km) away. By the end of the war in 1945, the *Enterprise* and its planes had sunk 72 ships and had destroyed 911 planes. The *Enterprise* proved that aircraft carriers and carrier technology were key to winning a war away from home.

The Enterprise *(sailing here during World War II) was 827 feet (252.1 m) long and could carry 96 planes. In 1943, the* Enterprise, *called Big E, was the first carrier to use its aircraft in nighttime attacks.*

The Flight Deck

A carrier's flight deck is much shorter than an airport runway, so a steam-powered machine called a **catapult** is used to help planes get up to speed for takeoff. The catapult was invented in 1915. Today an aircraft carrier has four catapults. It also usually has four steel wires to help planes land. A hook on the plane, called a tail hook, grabs one of the wires as the plane lands, stopping it. If the wires fail to stop the plane, the plane needs to be traveling fast enough to take off again so that it can come back for another landing.

The control tower, or island, is located on the flight deck. The bridge is a room in the control tower from which the captain controls the ship. Also in the control tower is the area called the **primary** flight control, or pri-fly, from which all commands for flight activity are given.

Top: *A control tower has radar, the primary flight control, and the captain's bridge.*
Bottom: *As do most modern carriers, the USS* Carl Vinson *has an angled deck. This enables a plane to land while other planes prepare to take off on the other end of the flight deck. If a plane cannot land safely, the angled deck allows it to take off again.*

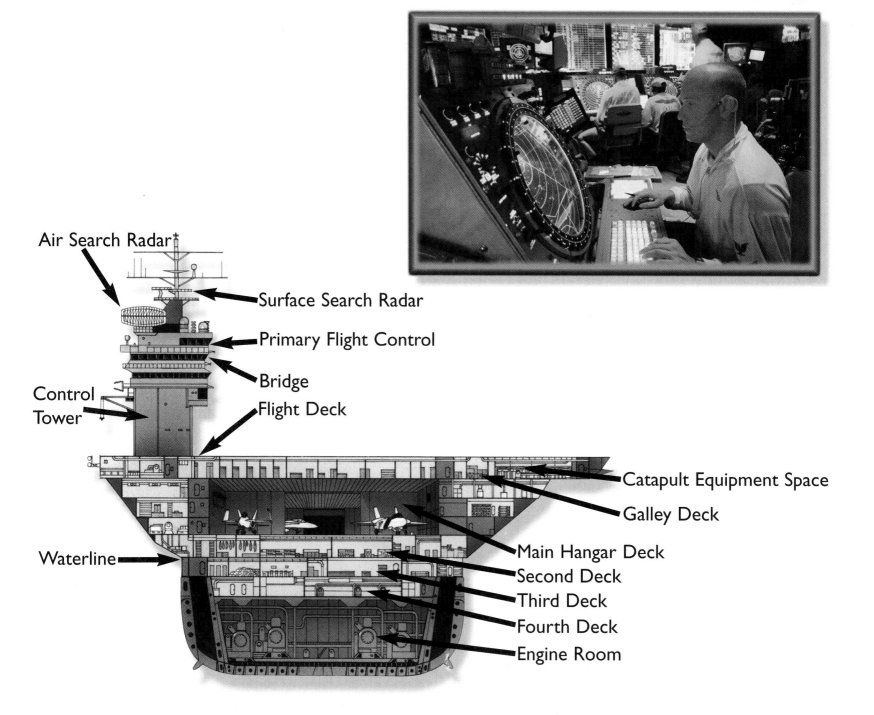

Air Search Radar

Surface Search Radar

Primary Flight Control

Bridge

Control Tower

Flight Deck

Catapult Equipment Space

Galley Deck

Waterline

Main Hangar Deck

Second Deck

Third Deck

Fourth Deck

Engine Room

The Lower Decks

Everything below the flight deck is called the lower decks, or below. About 60 planes can be stored below in an area called the hangar. The hangars in today's aircraft carriers are 685 feet (208.8 m) long, 110 feet (33.5 m) wide, and 25 feet (7.6 m) high. When the planes are needed, they are brought to the flight deck on one of four elevators. Behind the hangar and near the rear of the ship, there are areas where the crew can test and repair aircraft engines. In the lower decks, crew members sleep, eat, and relax when they are not on duty.

Carriers have rooms in the lower decks called engine rooms. Engine rooms contain machines called boilers, which make steam. Carriers use steam to power the engines. The engines turn propellers, or screws, which are machines with blades that move carriers through the water.

Top: *The USS* Enterprise's *carrier air traffic control center, which keeps track of aircraft that are not on the carrier but are in the region, is located below the flight deck.*
Bottom: *This cutaway view shows the supercarrier USS* Harry S. Truman *from the front. The carrier, which began service in 1998, can hold about 80 aircraft in its hangars.*

Supercarriers

Supercarriers are the biggest carriers in the world. The first supercarrier was the USS *Forrestal*, which entered service in 1955. The United States began making supercarriers shortly after jet planes were invented. Jets need more space to land because they land at higher speeds. They also use greater amounts of fuel than earlier planes, which means the carriers need more space for storage.

In 1961, the supercarrier USS *Enterprise* entered into military service. It is the eighth U.S. ship to bear this name. This *Enterprise* is 1,123 feet (342.3 m) long. Its flight deck is 4 ½ acres (1.8 ha) in area. It has a crew of about 6,000. The *Enterprise* is the first supercarrier to be run with **nuclear power**. The eight **nuclear reactors** that power the *Enterprise* can create enough energy for the ship to run for about 13 years without making a stop.

The USS Enterprise, *whose flight deck is shown here, has 4 catapults and about 85 aircraft. Nuclear-powered supercarriers are sometimes called floating cities. They have stores, barbershops, churches, post offices, and even bank machines.*

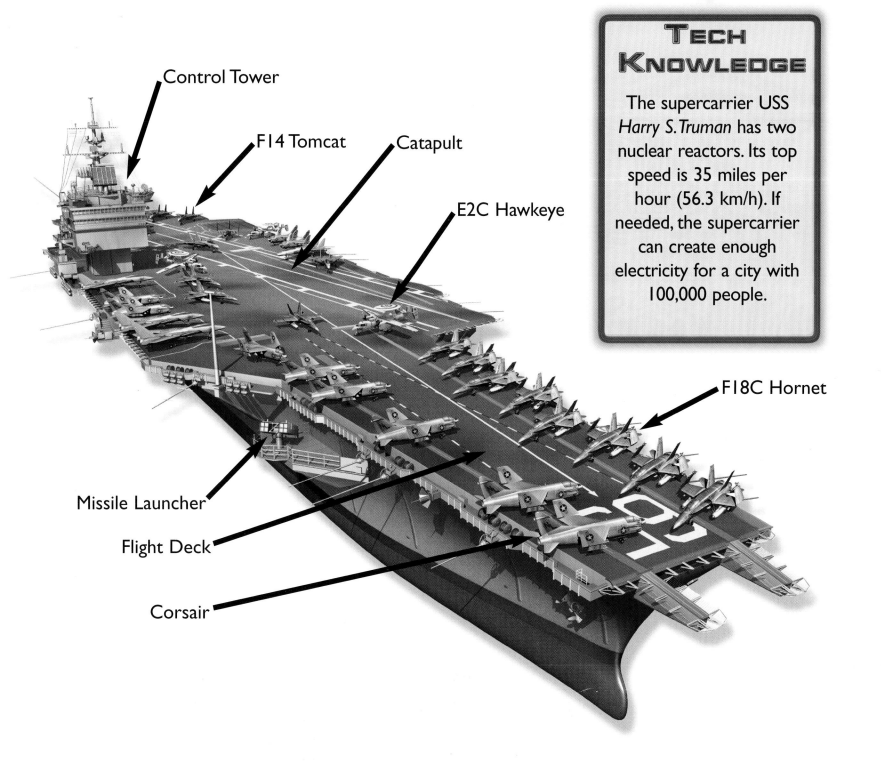

Control Tower

F14 Tomcat

Catapult

E2C Hawkeye

F18C Hornet

Missile Launcher

Flight Deck

Corsair

Building an Aircraft Carrier

Ships are built in a dry dock. The dry dock is not filled with water until the ship is able to float. The only company with a dry dock big enough to build supercarriers for the United States is Northrop Grumman Newport News in Newport News, Virginia. The Northrop Grumman dry dock is close to the James River.

A crane capable of lifting 900 tons (816.5 t) is used to put the carrier together. The crane lowers about 40 large steel sections into place, one by one. Then workers weld, or melt, them together. Once the keel, or the bottom of the ship, is complete, workers lower into place about 200 prebuilt **compartments** called superlifts. A superlift might contain many rooms, extending above and below several decks. After about five years of building and testing, the carrier is ready to sail.

The dry dock in Newport News that is used to build supercarriers is called Dry Dock 12. Dry Dock 12 is seen here when the carrier USS Ronald Reagan was being built, around 2000. Measuring 1,613 feet (491.6 m) long, 250 feet (76.2 m) wide, and 32 feet (9.8 m) deep, Dry Dock 12 is one of the largest dry docks in the world.

17

The Air Wing

Supercarriers can carry from 80 to 90 planes. The planes on a carrier are called the air wing. Most aircraft carriers transport several kinds of planes. Fighter planes, such as the Hornet and the Tomcat, are quick jets used to attack enemy targets and to protect the aircraft carrier. Planes, such as the Viking, and **helicopters**, including the Seahawk, are used to search for and to battle enemy **submarines**. Some planes, such as the Hawkeye, are used to improve the carrier's radar system so that it can be better prepared for an attack. Radar technology is used to learn the position and the speed of an object. Because the Hawkeye can fly as high as 25,000 feet (7,620 m) above the carrier, it is more effective at spotting enemy planes than is the carrier's radar system.

Top: *The SH-60 Seahawk helicopter is used for hunting enemy submarines and for search and rescue operations.* Middle: *The S-3B Viking has special radar to track and to coordinate attacks on enemy submarines.* Bottom: *The EA-6B Prowler uses special equipment to block an enemy's radar and communications systems during a battle.*

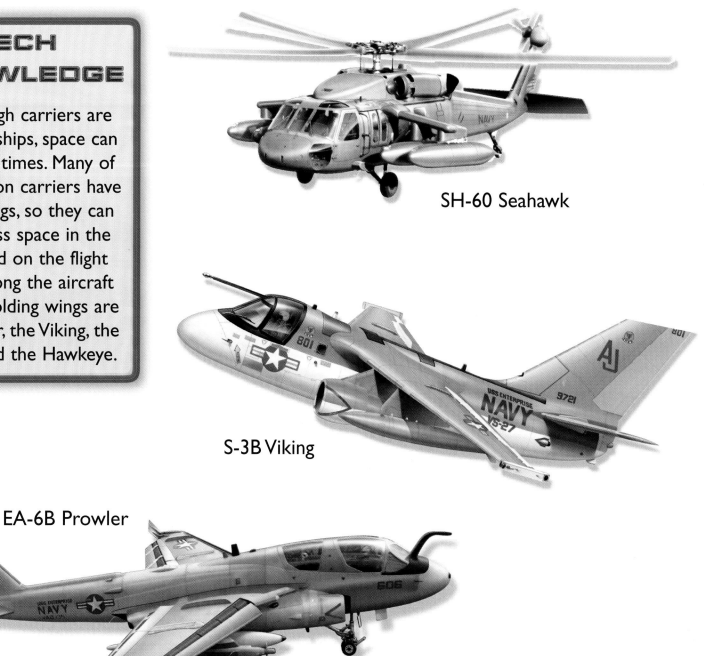

TECH KNOWLEDGE

Even though carriers are very large ships, space can be tight at times. Many of the planes on carriers have folding wings, so they can take up less space in the hangar and on the flight deck. Among the aircraft that have folding wings are the Prowler, the Viking, the Tomcat, and the Hawkeye.

SH-60 Seahawk

S-3B Viking

EA-6B Prowler

TIMELINE

1903 The Wright brothers make the first successful airplane flight.

1910 American pilot Eugene Ely takes off from the USS *Birmingham*.

1922 The USS *Jupiter* becomes the first U.S. aircraft carrier, USS *Langley*.

1933 The USS *Ranger*, the first U.S. aircraft carrier designed as such, is built.

1938 The USS *Enterprise* begins military service.

1939–1945 The *Enterprise* is the most active and successful U.S. aircraft carrier used during World War II.

1955 The first supercarrier, the USS *Forrestal*, begins service.

1961 The longest supercarrier, the USS *Enterprise*, begins service.

1998 The USS *Harry S. Truman* begins service.

2001 The USS *Ronald Reagan*, the ninth nuclear-powered aircraft carrier, is launched and is expected to join the U.S. Navy's fleet in 2003.

Flight Operations

Crews who fly, maintain, and organize aircraft activities are also part of the air wing. The leader of the air wing crew, the air boss, watches the flight deck from the control tower. The aircraft handling officer helps the air boss to direct the movement of all planes on the flight deck. The hangar deck officer directs the movement of aircraft in the hangar. Both of these officers, along with many other crew members, keep in close contact with the air boss at all times to make sure all operations run smoothly.

To make it easy for people to identify members of the flight deck crew, crew members wear different colors, depending on what their job is. For example, people with yellow shirts direct the movement of planes. People wearing blue shirts drive the tractors that move planes. The catapult officer, or the shooter, leads the members of the catapult crew, who wear green shirts.

Flight deck directors, or yellow shirts, guide the movement of planes on the flight deck. The flight deck director in this photo is giving hand signals to the pilot of a Prowler with folding wings to help guide the pilot to the correct spot for getting on or off the elevator.

Aircraft Carriers of the Future

The United States has airplanes called **stealth** bombers and stealth fighters. These aircraft have special shapes and are made with special **materials** that make them hard to locate by radar. The United States plans to use these planes on carriers. They are also planning to use stealth technology to build carriers. At present, it is impossible to hide completely ships as large as skyscrapers from radar. However, these special materials can make stealth carriers appear smaller than they really are.

New carriers will also have **automated** systems. Machines will do some of the tasks that people currently do. Radar systems and weapons-loading systems are two of the areas that may soon be automated. Automated systems will cut down the number of people needed to run carriers. Fewer crew members means lower operating costs and the loss of fewer lives during battles.

Glossary

automated (AH-tuh-mayt-ed) Operating without help.

biplanes (BY-playnz) Early airplanes that had two pairs of wings placed one above the other.

catapult (KA-tuh-pult) A machine that pushes a plane along a runway to help it gain speed for takeoff.

compartments (kum-PART-ments) Separate sections of something.

converted (kun-VERT-ed) Changed something into a different form.

helicopters (HEH-luh-kop-terz) Aircraft that are kept in the air by blades that spin above the craft.

materials (muh-TEER-ee-ulz) What objects are made of.

monoplanes (MAH-noh-playnz) Airplanes with only one pair of wings.

nuclear power (NOO-klee-ur POW-ur) A type of power that uses the energy that exists in the nucleus, or center, of an atom, which is the smallest bit of matter. It is created by splitting atoms or by forcing the centers of certain atoms together.

nuclear reactors (NOO-klee-ur ree-AK-turz) Machines in which nuclear power is safely created.

primary (PRY-mer-ee) Main; greatest in importance.

radar (RAY-dar) A machine that uses sound waves or radio waves to locate objects.

seaplanes (SEE-playnz) Airplanes that have special floats for taking off from and landing on water.

stealth (STELTH) Secret, sneaky movement.

submarines (SUB-muh-reenz) Ships that are designed to travel underwater.

technology (tek-NAH-luh-jee) The way that a people do something using tools, and the tools that they use.

transport (TRANZ-port) To move something from one place to another.

Index

A
air wing, 18, 21

C
catapults, 10
control tower, 10

D
dry dock, 17

F
flight deck(s), 5, 10, 13, 21

H
hangars, 13, 21

L
lower decks, 13

N
nuclear power, 14
nuclear reactors, 14

R
radar, 9, 18, 22
runway(s), 5, 10

S
supercarriers, 14, 17–18
superlifts, 17

U
U.S. Navy, 5, 9
USS *Enterprise*, 9, 14
USS *Forrestal*, 14
USS *Jupiter*, 5
USS *Langley*, 5–6
USS *Lexington*, 5
USS *Saratoga*, 5

W
World War I, 6
World War II, 6, 9
Wright brothers, 6

Web Sites

Due to the changing nature of Internet links, PowerKids Press has developed an online list of Web sites related to the subject of this book. This site is updated regularly. Please use this link to access the list:
www.powerkidslinks.com/kgit/aircraft/